KNOW
WHO
YOU
ARE

A SPIRITUAL GUIDE TO
ERADICATING ANXIETY, DEPRESSION,
——— AND DIS-EASE ———

KNOW
WHO
YOU
ARE

A SPIRITUAL GUIDE TO
ERADICATING ANXIETY, DEPRESSION,
—— AND DIS-EASE ——

COURTNEY MARTIN

360 TRAINING INSTITUTE
CHICAGO, IL

KNOW WHO YOU ARE
A SPIRITUAL GUIDE TO ERATICATING
ANXIETY, DEPRESSION, AND DIS-EASE

ISBN-13: 978-0-578-70273-5

360 Training Institute
Chicago, IL

Printed in the United States of America
First Edition August 2020

Design: Make Your Mark Publishing Solutions
Editing: Make Your Mark Publishing Solutions
Illustrations: Erin Kelly

Acknowledgements

I would like to first thank God, my Father, the God in me. Thank you, Jesus. Thank you for the strength, guidance, and inspiration to write and share my experiences and ideas. Thanks to all my parents, children, brothers, sisters, cousins, nieces, and nephews for your continued support and unconditional love. Thank you, Aunt Margaret. Your display of strength and endurance is inspiring. Thank you to my finest student, Jeremiah. "Mid-range all day!" It's inspiring the way you listen and apply. I learn from you. You always figure it out, and it always works out for you. You keep me on top of my game because I have to lead by example, and at any given time I can ask myself, "What would I tell J?" A special thanks to Valarie. Thank you to Monique D. Mensah, my personal self-publishing assistant, with Make Your Mark Publishing Solutions. I couldn't have done it without you. The process was made easy, and all I had to do was create. Your services are amazing! Thank you to all my friends and family. You all helped me at some point for me to get to this point. I appreciate it!

Dedication

To my cousin Lavi Williams

*My good friend Clifford "Skinny" Moore, who was
murdered from gun violence in Chicago as I was
finishing Chapter 5: "Peace, Joy, and Happiness."*

*Anyone suffering from PTSD, depression,
anxiety, autoimmune disease, or any ailment.*

This book is a seed. Plant (read) it and watch it grow. Watch the harvest. There is a gestation period—some longer than others, some immediate. Keep planting. Keep watering.

Contents

Introduction

Truth > Facts

"The beginning of wisdom is: Acquire wisdom, and with all your acquiring, get understanding." (Prov. 4:7 NASB)

It may be a fact that you have symptoms of sickness or poverty, that your life isn't where you want it to be, or you just don't feel well. But there is another way, a greater way—the truth! Once you become aware that the truth is greater than facts, you can reclaim what is rightfully yours. The "facts"of life won't affect you anymore, and you can live your truth. Peace, love, success, health, happiness, joy, prosperity, wealth, and all your heart's desires belong to you. That's the truth. Whether or not you currently possess them is unimportant; they are yours. In fact, if you possess anything other than those things, you are walking around with stolen property. Give it back and redeem what is rightfully yours. You just have to know the laws of the truth and operate within them to claim what's yours.

What does it mean to say the truth is greater than the facts? It may be a fact that you feel physically ill, anxious, depressed, or poor. The truth is you were promised some things on this earth, but you have to have the wisdom, understanding, and knowledge to obtain those promises, to claim what's rightfully yours. Some of us were never told this, so we have been made subject to things that may be fact but certainly are not true. This lack of knowledge has made you vulnerable to sickness, depression, lack, and many other things that don't inherently belong to you. This doesn't define you, nor is it who you really are.

This book will help you identify and define who you really are. It will help you permanently live in your truth. The only things you lack are knowledge, wisdom, and understanding, and this lack has caused you to believe, act, and live below your true God-given nature and ability, without your God-given rights and possessions. That changes right now! You have the right to enjoy life and live it more abundantly in all things—joy, happiness, success, peace, love, health, and wealth. If you aren't living abundantly, you are reading this book at the exact right time.

The universe we live in is governed by laws, just like any city, state, country, or land where you reside. These laws allow you to know what you are entitled to. They regulate your actions and let you know the benefits or consequences of them. Laws give you the appropriate procedures or behaviors.When you don't know the law, you are leaving the door open to be taken advantage of. I am sure you are somewhat aware of the basic laws that govern your town, school, or job, so why don't you know the universal laws? You must become aware of them. Wouldn't knowing these universal laws make it easier to navigate through *any* land, circumstance, or situation? When you have a solid knowledge and understanding of these universal laws, you will begin to understand yourself. If you understand why and how you operate and do the things you do, you will begin to understand others.

Have you ever done something without knowing why you did it? Have you ever asked a kid why they did something and they said, "I don't know"? It may sound silly, but they could be telling the truth. Chances are people really don't know why they do what they do or why they feel the way they feel. I am going to help you with that. After reading this book, you will know why you feel the way you do or why you behave the way you do. The purpose of this book is to provide you with wisdom and understanding. It doesn't matter how religious you are, you're lost unless you learn how to use your mind. It doesn't matter how much formal education someone has; a man is ignorant until he learns how to use his mind. The proper use of your mind will enable you to do, have, and *be* the good you desire. This will renew your mind.

"And do not be conformed to this world, but be transformed by the renewing of your mind." (Rom. 12:2)

Learning how to properly use your mind will stir up your true self, bringing into remembrance some truths you may have forgotten. How did you forget? That happens through your environment, how you were raised, and the people you're around the most. What you take in with your eyes and ears—TV, radio, internet, media, or any idol words—shape your beliefs, which then affect your actions. This renewing of the mind will raise your level of conscious awareness far above any sickness, disease, depression, or poverty.

What is conscious awareness? Have you ever rented a car or knew someone who bought a new car? Suddenly, you start seeing that same kind of car every day on the road, when you never noticed it before. Well, that's because you have been made consciously aware that the car exists because you experienced it with your senses. It had always been there, but your new level of awareness made it visible. With visualization, you can experience anything you want without the senses and bring it into your world, but that's for another chapter.

By reading this book, you will experience truths and ideas through your senses just as you experienced that car, and it will consciously raise your awareness so you can see things in this world that already exist, like peace, love, joy, happiness, prosperity, wealth, and success. You have to become aware to be able to change. The solutions to your problems are already here; they're just on a higher level of awareness. Being worried, anxious, angry, depressed, or frustrated are low-level emotions, and solutions don't reside there. This book will lift you up and take you higher. It will give you wisdom and understanding and the tools and abilities to rise up and overcome any problem. These aren't all my ideas, but I have tested them. Now I'm delivering the information and reminding you of what your true self already knows. That is why certain statements will resonate with you and evoke emotion and higher thoughts. Truth recognizes truth; some may say real recognizes real.

Take these words as friendly reminders. It's all about awareness. Being aware of the information and knowledge I am going to share with you is vital and life changing. This is the real work that must be done. The internal work is the road to freedom. If you do not like what you see on the outside, it's time to look under the hood and fix the inside. Whatever's happening on the outside is just a reflection of the inside; it's the one thing all religions and all great people agree on. "As a man thinketh, so he is" (Prov. 23:7). You are what you constantly think about and speak of. I will give you the understanding of speaking in later chapters. What you think and what you speak every moment of your life is key in shaping your future. It is key to your peace, happiness, and the way you feel. Thinking and speaking the right way is a daily practice. It is righteousness. Be a professional, not an amateur. A professional does it for a living every day, not just a couple days out of the week; there are no days off. Every great musician, physician, artist, or athlete who has made it to the top of their profession has done so through hours of daily practice, repetition, focus, will, imagination, discipline, trial, and error. The same will be required of you to strengthen your mind and these faculties to achieve the pinnacles of success and rewards of a long, healthy life.

Who You Are (Spirit, Mind, Body)

First, we must understand who we are. Chances are you don't know who you really are. If you are going to change anything in your life, you must understand who you really are. We exist on three different levels of understanding. First, we are spirit beings; second, we have an intellect (mind, imagination, will, and emotions), and third, we live in a body. There is a universal power that resides in all of us, which is the spirit; our bodies don't exist without it. I will get to the intellect later. If the spirit is removed from the body, it falls, becomes motionless, and lies dormant. This can be called physical death—no spirit within, no life in the body. That means everything starts with the spirit.

That spirit or life force within doesn't know lack, sickness, or fear. It is love. It is good. It is creative. It is all-knowing and an ever-present help. It is powerful. It is unchanging. It is eternal. It is faithful. It is truth. It protects. It is a provider, an infinite supply. It is sufficient. It is health. It is infinite, unlimited, and abundant. I can go on forever, but if you know that's what you are equipped with on the inside, that should be enough to proceed. It is referred to as God, "I Am," the Oneness, the Infinite, Source, or the Creator. I will probably refer to Him as all of these throughout this book—whichever fits best to get the point across. Feel free to substitute any of these words if it helps you understand or advance your learning.

This spirit being that resides in you is perfect. You may ask, "Why do things happen to me? Why am I sick? Why am I anxious or depressed? Why am I hurting? Why am I broke?" Well, there is a good chance your intellect (mind, imagination, will, and emotions) has gotten in the way of this beautiful, perfect spirit flowing through you to deliver the good you and your body deserve or desire. The intellect has to be trained and, oftentimes, renewed to obtain the health, wealth, happiness, peace, joy, and success that is rightfully yours.

Have you ever seen someone who was very smart intellectually but down on their luck? That can be an example of the intellect getting in the way. It's a low level of consciousness but a high intellect. You have to learn how to get in tune and make all three work together. Just like any electronic device, it doesn't work unless you plug it into the source, usually an outlet that is powered by electricity. You can't see the electrical energy used to power the device, but you plug it in because you believe in the power. You believe that once you plug in your device, that power will flow. The same thing applies here: You can't see the spirit inside of you, but once you believe it's there, you can plug in the exact same way. And when you're plugged in and all three are aligned—spirit, mind, and body—you are in harmony.

We must learn to live in harmony. This is achieved by learning the correct way to think and use of our imagination. Most of our suffering—whether it's mental or physical—stems from the misuse of our mind or imagination. Everything starts with a thought or image. When you raise a finger, leg, or make any physical movement, it's because you thought about it first. Whether you are conscious of it or not, every movement your body makes is first made in thought. This is an example of cause and effect, which happens to be one of the laws of the universe. For anything to happen (the effect), there first must be a cause. The cause is your thought. The effect is your actions or result. No matter the situation, part of being consciously aware is being aware of your thoughts. Every thought. Every moment. It is imperative, and your life depends on it. Why? Because your thoughts affect your life. Time after time, we are reminded how to think.

"Finally, brethren, whatever is true, whatever is honorable, whatever is right, whatever is pure, whatever is lovely, whatever is of good repute, if there is any excellence and if anything worthy of praise, dwell on these things." (Phil. 4:8)

So if our thoughts and imagination are the cause of every movement and effect in the body and our outer world (sickness, depression, or poverty), we need to know how our inner world works. We need to get under the hood, look at the manual, and see how the intellect or our mind operates. If you don't know how your mind operates, how can you make improvements to your thoughts?

Most people take their car to a mechanic when the check engine light comes on or when it's time for maintenance because the mechanic knows the inner workings of that car. Mechanics know the product inside and out; they know how it operates and what to do to get it running efficiently. Well, I am the mechanic for your mind. I know its inner workings and will give you the tools to keep you running like new.

> **Perceived fact:** *"It runs in my family. It's in my DNA. I grew up like this."*

> **Truth:** *"God created man in His own image, in the image of God He created him; male and female He created them." (Gen.1:27)*

Your spirit within you is perfect. Once you let that sink into your consciousness, your DNA will become like God. No one is in control of you, your health, destiny, or promise. Don't let the intellect tell you otherwise. The intellect is simply sending you information from past experience. This is a new experience, and sometimes new thoughts and ideas take some convincing and getting used to. It has been scientifically proven that we can rewire our brains and change our DNA with positive thoughts, words, and actions.

> *"For as he thinks in his heart, so is he." (Prov. 23:7)*

How do you think in your heart? I'm not referring to the physical heart that is pumping in your chest but, rather, your subconscious mind or your general belief system.

> *"It shall be done to you according to your faith." (Matt 9:29)*

That verse can also be translated to say "Whatever a man believes, he is." As you can see, everything hinges upon the truth that whatever you believe or have faith in is what you are. You obtain a belief from thinking the same thing over and over again. You obtain faith by hearing over and over again. Being consciously aware of what you think and hear on a consistent basis is very important because it shapes your beliefs.

Humans mostly think in pictures. If I ask you what a tennis ball looks like, you'll automatically picture a tennis ball in your head. If I ask you what your bed looks like, you automatically picture yourself in your bedroom. You can picture the doorway and anything that's in it. So how does your mind look?

Did a picture of the brain pop up? I'm sure because when I was first introduced to this idea, that's what popped up in my head. But the brain and the mind are two separate things. If we think in pictures, how are we going to change our results and the way we think if we don't have an image of the mind? You have no way of recognizing what the mind looks like; you have no reference point—until now! I am going to present you with the image that was introduced to me by a great mentor of mine, Bob Proctor.

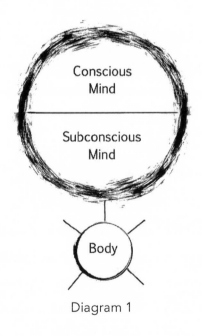

Diagram 1

This image came from Dr. Thurman Fleet, who presented it in San Antonio in 1934. Seeing this image changed my life and gave me a greater understanding of not only myself but others as well. People all look and behave differently, but we are all of the same nature. This doctor understood that we had to get to the root of the problem (the cause) to make permanent changes.

In the healing arts, professionals mostly treat the physical symptoms. But until we start to treat the whole person, there won't be any permanent change. The true cause is in the mind. What goes on in the body is merely an effect or a manifestation of what's been going on in the mind. Remember, the body cannot do anything without the mind telling it to first. Our way of thinking has to be healed. The way we speak has to be retrained. This is why people remain in their state of misfortune for years or even a lifetime and pass it on for generations. But it's possible to get to the point where you learn how to give your body a command and it obeys you. The body is the lowest in the chain of command.

The information brought forth by a new way of

thinking can be passed down for generations and you can begin to control your destiny instead of just living by chance and the lies that are offered to you. If you are ready to make changes in your life, I suggest you repeatedly study this diagram and this book, and if needed, contact me for greater understanding.

If you are depressed, lacking something, have a disease, or suffering from something as minor as the common cold, those are just external symptoms letting you know that something isn't in alignment within. Your check engine light is on. The inner self is perfect. It doesn't know sickness, depression, or lack. If you treat the root of the problem— the cause—you will get permanent change and you won't have to worry about sickness, disease, poverty, or despondency anymore. Your mind is one hundred times more powerful than any computer on the planet. You have enough electrical power within you to light up a city. Learn how to upgrade your mental software so you can have the good you desire. What happens when you don't upgrade your phone? It starts tripping, right? Upgrade your mind now!

2

I Am (Unconditional Love/True Self)

God is the great I Am.

> "...'What is His name? What shall I say to them?' God said to Moses, 'I AM WHO I AM'; and He said, 'Thus you shall say to the sons of Israel, 'I AM has sent me to you.'" (Exod. 3:13-14)

> "Cease striving and know that I am God..." (Ps. 46:10)

> "...for I am God, and there is no other." (Isa. 46:9)

"I am" says "I am God." "I am" is the awareness of being. You are announcing your awareness by saying, "I am..." So "I am," or the awareness of being, creates everything (I am God/Creator). You become or create everything you say, think, believe, or feel after "I am." After "I am," only speak the good you desire because God (I Am) is good. If it isn't good, then it's not from God and doesn't belong to you. You must learn the promises of good. This will give you the ability to recognize a lie and replace it with truth, with good. You must deny the symptoms, the lies offered to you, and only speak and think the truth.

> *"My people are destroyed for lack of knowledge." (Hosea 4:6)*

The Spirit or the I Am that dwells within you doesn't lack health, happiness, or wealth. The only thing you lack is knowledge. Once you *know* or have knowledge of the truth, the truth will set you free from all worry, sickness, anxiety, depression, brokenness, or suffering. If you don't have something, whether it's love, happiness, wealth, or anything you desire, it is because you either don't have the awareness or knowledge to free yourself or you haven't aligned with it yet. Everything is already here available for us—the health, happiness, peace, joy, and wealth we desire. You are a spirit being that lives in a body. There is an infinite force within you that controls the outer world. The spirit controls the physical. You have to learn how to align with the divine spirit within first, so all things are added unto you.

> *"But seek first His kingdom and His rightoeousness, and all these things will be added to you." (Matt. 6:33)*

> *"Beloved, I pray that in all respects you may prosper and be in good health, just as your soul prospers." (3 John 2)*

If there is something wrong or lacking on the outside, your job is to fix something on the inside. Nurture your soul (mind, will, imagination, and focus), and you are promised to have prosperity and good health, including mental health. But you have to know the truth. And once you know the truth, you will be free and equipped to fight for and keep your freedom.

Alignment with unconditional love (I Am) is a major key in obtaining the good you want to be and have. What does unconditional love mean? It means that no outside conditions or circumstances can change the love. What is love? God is love. God is good. He never changes. That means love is within you and with you every moment. It is closer than you think, closer than the breaths you take. Love will never leave you nor forsake you. He loves you no matter what condition you are in or the circumstances surrounding you. You are God's (love) child. This is the greatest love of all: a father and His child.

One of the most famous children of God is Yeshua or Jesus. Jesus is the greatest mastermind in God's consciousness. He consciously knew He was God's child. Jesus is God's mind in man. Jesus became so conscious of God that when He spoke, God spoke. This is why He was able to perform miracles and wonders and display instant manifestations as a man walking the earth. He spoke to a fig tree, and it withered and died in twenty-four hours (Mark 11:12-25). He spoke to the wind, and it ceased (Matt. 8:23-27). We must become conscious of the I Am, the power within us, just as Jesus did. It is the same power that created heaven and earth, and it resides in you. You must develop a personal relationship with this power within. God has to become personal in you, through you, and as you. It makes it easier to emulate, ask, receive, learn, and understand someone you have a relationship with.

> *"Believe Me that I am in the Father and the Father is in Me; otherwise believe because of the works themselves. Truly, truly, I say to you, he who believes in Me, the works that I do, he will also do; and greater works than these he will do; because I go to the Father." (John 14:11-12)*

To do the works the master did, you must have the same mindset or consciousness. Then, you will possess the master power, which will give you the desires of your heart. You must believe that the Father, I Am, Source, and/or Creator is in you and you in Him. You must become one. This may knock your socks off, but the only difference between Jesus and everyone else is pure consciousness. Jesus is God's son, and He knows that. A man is God's son also; he just doesn't know it yet. This is why He says you shall know the truth (that you are the son/child of God), and the truth shall make you free. It sets you free from all the lies of sickness, disease, and depression. No child of the most high is subject to that because what parent would want their child to be sick or lacking? God only wants what's good for you. Love, well-being, and peace is your true nature. This is to be born again with a renewed mind. You are born again from humanity into divinity.

"Abide in Me, and I in you. As the branch cannot bear fruit of itself unless it abides in the vine, so neither can you unless you abide in Me. I am the vine, you are the branches; he who abides in Me and I in him, he bears much fruit, for apart from Me you can do nothing." (John 15:4-5)

Abide: *To remain stable or fixed in a state. To continue in a place. (Merriam Webster Dictionary)*

You have to learn how to abide with love and goodness. Believe in your own divine rights as a child of God. To abide with goodness and love is the same as agreeing with God. God is love. God is good. Being in agreement with good takes faith. Faith is trust. You must have faith or trust that good is with you and expect that good is working for you, even if the situation appears to be bad. Trust that love will never fail you and is always with you. The opposite of faith is fear. Faith and fear are the same type of force. They both require you to believe in something. They are both expectations, both feelings, and they both attract—just polar opposites. I will get more into feelings in later chapters.

Faith and fear cannot occupy the same space. If faith is present, fear has to disappear, and vice versa. How do you develop your faith? "Faith comes by hearing, and by hearing the word of God; *words of good, words of love*" (Rom.10:17). How does fear come? Since it's the opposite of faith, it comes the same way: by hearing bad reports or seeing bad images, which can come from friends, family, the environment, or the media. Fear is the *root* cause of any anxiety, depression, or suffering.

> *"My son, give attention to my words; incline your ear to my sayings."* (Prov. 4:20)

You must be conscious of everything you see or hear. Remember, the heart is the subjective/subconscious mind. This is serious business because it will determine how you feel, which then determines your beliefs and actions. "Watch over your heart with all diligence, for from it flow the springs of life" (Prov. 4:23). The way you feel is just a result of what you have been believing, seeing, speaking, thinking, and hearing. The word of God is called the gospel, which means the good.

> *"In the beginning was the Word, and the Word was with God, and the Word was God." (John 1:1)*

As you see, God and His word are one. Also remember, God is good, God is love (1 John 4:8), so you can substitute God, good, love, and word and reread the verses for a greater understanding.

> *"In the beginning was good/love, and the good/love was with good/love, and the good/love was good/love."*

That's pretty amazing when you substitute the words and really think about it. Attend to the love/good/God/word. Listen to the love/good/God/word and don't let it depart from your eyes. Keep it in your mind. As you can see, you have to be diligent. It's going to take some discipline because every moment counts, and there are distractions and things that don't serve you that are fighting for your attention. This is why you must stay focused on good and love at all times. At any given moment, you are either operating in love or fear; there is no in between. You must be aware of the cause of your emotions, thoughts, words, or actions because they affect your results in life. Anything that is not the nature of love has to be avoided.

Now, allow me to help you understand the nature of love (God) or good so you may fully understand your true nature. "Love is patient, love is kind. It does not envy, it does not boast, it is not proud. It does not dishonor others, it is not self-seeking, it is not easily angered, it keeps no record of wrongs. Love does not delight in evil but rejoices with the truth. It always protects, always trusts, always hopes, always perseveres. Love never fails." (1Cor. 13:4-8) This is the blueprint for alignment with good and love. These are the qualities you should walk in to be successful, healthy, and prosperous. If you apply the truths and principles stated in this book, you will be in vibrational alignment with love, peace, joy, and perfect health. All things will be under your feet—above and not beneath, the head and not the tail. You will ascend so high that problems, sicknesses, and diseases will not be able to exist in your world and will fall far away from your life permanently. If something does try to attack you, this will give you the training to stay calm in the midst of a battle. Being calm shows trust. Trust that the victory is always yours. Love wants you to be healthy, sees you healthy, and has already made you healthy. You just need to know the love. God is love, and love never fails, so God never fails. God is within you.

> "...For behold, the kingdom of God is
> in your midst." (Luke 17:21)

Once you become aware that God is within you and is not just some man in the sky, you will begin to step into your true power.

Speak It into Existence

Confession (Speaking and Decreeing)

> "Death and life are in the power of the tongue..." (Prov. 18:21)

> "...You have been snared with the words of your mouth..." (Prov. 6:2)

> "Let the words of my mouth and the meditation of my heart be acceptable in your sight." (Ps. 19:14)

> "For by your words you shall be justified..." (Matt. 12:37)

Continually, we are advised of the power of words. Certainly, people are aware you can speak things into existence. We say it all the time, more as a cliché than anything else. But did you know this law is in effect twenty-four seven? Many seem to think it only applies to the good things they desire, but death and life are both in the power of the tongue. If your tongue can be used to speak positivity, life, or blessings, surely the same applies for negativity, death, and curses. We can start from the very beginning. Creation was made with a spoken word.

> *"In the beginning God created the heavens and the earth. The earth was formless and void... Then God SAID, 'Let there be light'; and there was light." (Gen. 1:1-3)*

Now, we have already established that God and His power are within us, so this means you possess that same creative power when you speak. Even when the earth was only darkness and void, God didn't panic, He simply spoke what He wanted.

In the book of Genesis, every time God wanted something, He said, "Let there be…" and it was. Where did the light come from? God is the father of light. He says He is the light of the world. He was able to say "Let there be light" because that's what was in Him and that's what He is. You can only create from your own consciousness. Become what you want to be on the inside so you will have the ability to manifest it on the outside and see the results you desire. You have the same ability. No matter how dark it gets, no matter how empty and void it seems, you have the power within you to change what you see by simply speaking. You have been made aware that I Am is God, so anything you say after "I Am" has creative power.

> *"Let the weak say, 'I am a strong.'"*
> *(Joel 3:10)*

> **Perceived Fact:** *You have physical symptoms of sickness or disease.*

> **Truth:** *I Am (God), the power inside of you, is healthy (I Am healthy).*

"I am sick," "I am broke," "I am anxious," and "I am depressed" do not exist to your true self or inner being. So no matter what your physical senses tell you, you must only affirm what you want and deny everything that doesn't line up with love. Call things that do not physically exist into existence. That is the way to redemption and deliverance. That is the way to peace and happiness. That is how you change the momentum of your fortune.

Before I proceed, let's be clear: To the God power within, curing cancer is just as easy as curing a cold.

> "It is as easy to create a button as a castle."
>
> —Abraham Hicks

> "Behold, I am the LORD, the God of all flesh; is anything too difficult for me?" (Jer. 32:27)

> "...With God, all things are possible." (Matt. 19:26)

It is only our human minds and conditioning that have made one greater than the other. But none is greater than the power within you, so it doesn't matter what the sickness or disease is. Mental or physical, these methods can be applied. Let's take the common cold for example, since I am sure you have experienced it.

You get a symptom that you may associate with a cold, such as a cough, runny nose, or sneezing. You get around a friend, co-worker, or even your own family member and cough, sneeze, and sniffle a few times, and what's the first question they often ask? "Are you catching a cold?" And before you know it, you say, "Yeah, I think I am getting sick." At that very moment, you just claimed something that didn't belong to you. You are a thief. The symptom and the question are being offered to you just to see if you will accept it, to see if you are more conscious of what you see or feel or more conscious of the God in you.

Nothing can be given to you without your permission. Do you think God gets sick? Would He say He is sick? You are using His name in vain by confessing "I am sick. I am catching..." Why would you want to catch a cold, anyway? You should be running from it. With that confession, you have just misplaced your faith in those symptoms or the sickness. "I am…" is the Creator, so whatever you put after it has to be created by law. Let's put this into perspective.

If FedEx or UPS came to your door with a package that didn't belong to you, would you sign for it? Most people wouldn't. You wouldn't claim that package because you don't want responsibility for what may be in the package, and it's against the law! So why take responsibility for a sickness that doesn't belong to you? Why claim it just because it was offered to you? This is breaking the law also.

Lie offered to you: *"Well, I have to tell it like it is."*

Truth: *No, you don't! If you tell it like it is, then that's how your situation will remain: the way it is. If you are already in a state of sickness or disease, you have to tell yourself and the universe how you want it to be—the truth! Speak deliverance and redemption.*

I am healthy! I am well! Speak life so you may have it more abundantly.

"Let the weak say, 'I am a strong.'" (Joel 3:10)

"You will also decree a thing, and it will be established for you; and the light will shine on your ways." (Job 22:28)

I have personally stopped symptoms in their tracks with these practices, by constantly affirming my divine right of perfect health. This comes with much practice, training, and lots of repetition. You have to constantly affirm you are healthy, well, and healed. You must affirm that all is well and give thanks for your health in every single moment, even if you have to say it a thousand times a day. Speak it until you believe it and see it in your life.

The consciousness of perfect health was planted in me just as I am doing for you. And once I fully received it, I haven't had to worry about any sickness, disease, or even something as "minor" as the common cold. As a teen, I had a boil that grew on my waistline. It became so painful and rock hard that I could hardly bend over to do anything, and I had to go to the emergency room. A doctor saw me and informed me that it was basically an infection. It was a good thing I came in. He stuck me with a needle and drained it. Nothing but puss and blood came out. After he was done, it immediately went down, and the pain subsided. Me being the curious person I am, I asked what would cause something like that. If I could prevent it from happening, I would like to know where I went wrong. That's just how I am; I hate preventable mistakes. He asked me if I ever got sick, and I said, "Maybe once a year, not often, though." That was a fact at that moment. So the physician told me the boil was a result of me not getting sick enough. It was a buildup that moved to one area and caused infection. Whether or not that assessment was true, I don't know. It sounded kind of weird to me, and it didn't resonate at all.

Fast forward a few months later, and I went to a seminar hosted by Dr. Bill Winston. Part of his message was that we don't have to accept the report of any doctor if it doesn't line up with the truth, no matter what the X-ray, scans, or reports physically show. The spirit controls the physical. He affirmed that we never have to get sick, not even once a year. He said those exact words. It was almost like he was talking directly to me. Now, this was music to my ears, and it made much more sense to me than what the physician had said in the past. From that day, I made the decision to never be sick, and I haven't been, and I am grateful.

Now that you are aware of how powerful your thoughts and words are, I am sure you will be much more careful about the way you speak about yourself or others. Why would anyone in their right mind ever say, "I am sick," "I am worthless," "I am depressed," "I am broke," "My feet are killing me," "This gets on my nerves," "I'm sick and tired," "It's a pain in the neck," "I'm under pressure," "This is hard"? I can go on for days with words and phrases that negatively shape our reality. Sometimes if you take a step back, you can even realize the exact point you spoke wrongly in a certain situation.

Again, if we can speak good into existence, surely it works for the opposite, the bad. Certainly God/good wouldn't say anything negative about Himself. After all, remember that I Am is the Creator. You are using His name in vain when you put anything bad after "I am…" Your body and the world around you have been created to respond to anything you put after "I am…" You are literally giving your body and the universe a command when you speak. Once you give a command, everything internally and spiritually goes to work to see that the word does not return void.

> *"…For I am watching over My word to perform it." (Jer. 1:12)*

This is why affirmations are so powerful and important. Always speak life, blessings, health, and wealth into your life, no matter how the conditions or circumstances may look. This is a part of practicing that unconditional love we discussed earlier. Every moment counts. Some may call it nitpicking, but this is your life. It depends on it; your future and your family depend on it. Your words have the creative power to turn any situation around in the blink of an eye. They have the power to turn darkness into light with a command.

With this newfound awareness, you will begin

to notice not only how you speak but how others speak. You will get to a point where those negative phrases will hurt and burn your ears. You will begin to realize if someone was truly thinking before they spoke, they wouldn't say half the things they do. I will be honest, this power has to be developed. It takes lots of repetition, discipline, and focus to break old habits. Most of the time, this type of training comes with the assistance of a coach. Every great champion has had a coach, trainer, or teacher at some point during their journey.

There have been studies with plants, which are living beings, that included a group of plants that were positively spoken to and a group that was negatively spoken to. The results showed that the plants spoken to in a loving, positive manner outlasted their counterparts.

There have also been studies done with water, which is interesting because the human body is roughly 70% water. The extraordinary life work of Dr. Emoto is documented in the New York Times Bestseller *The Hidden Messages in Water*. In his book, Dr. Emoto demonstrated how water exposed to loving, benevolent, and compassionate human intention resulted in aesthetically pleasing physical molecular formations in the water, while water exposed to fearful and discordant human intentions resulted in disconnected, disfigured, and "unpleasant" physical molecular formations. He did this through magnetic resonance analysis technology and high-speed photographs.

Take a look at the following water crystal photographs from Dr. Emoto's work. Each water crystal you see was exposed to the word that is written next to it prior to being photographed.

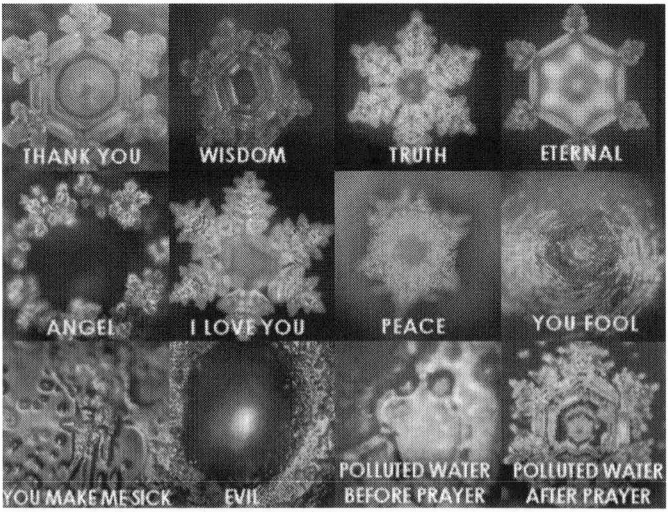
THANK YOU
WISDOM
TRUTH
ETERNAL
ANGEL
I LOVE YOU
PEACE
YOU FOOL
YOU MAKE ME SICK
EVIL
POLLUTED WATER BEFORE PRAYER
POLLUTED WATER AFTER PRAYER

www.thewellnessenterprise.com

It has been scientifically proven that negative thoughts and self-talk can cause brain damage over time. This was vital information to me because it let me know that I was in control. If I am in control, I refuse to cause myself harm. If I am in control, I can get the training, knowledge, wisdom, and understanding I need to live a healthy, wealthy, happy, joyous, peaceful, prosperous, and successful life.

Power of the Mind

Conscious/Subconscious
Seen and Unseen

> *"To think truth regardless of appearances is laborious and requires the expenditure of more power than any other work man is called upon to perform."*
>
> *—Wallace Wattles*

Everything is the result of a way of thinking, including success, peace, prosperity, health, and aging. So, according to the law of polarity, that means defeat, anxiety, depression, sickness, and poverty are also a result of a way of thinking. The invisible controls the visible. All of the power is in the unseen. Some of the most powerful forces on the earth cannot be seen, yet we acknowledge them. Can you see electricity? No, but you know it's there, and you plug into it as a source, with good faith it will charge your phone, toast your bread, curl your hair, and so on. How about wind? We cannot see actual wind, but we can recognize the effects it has when it blows. Ask anyone who lives in areas that are affected by hurricanes and typhoons.

> *"And there arose a fierce gale of wind, and the waves were breaking over the boat so much that the boat was already filling up. Jesus Himself was in the stern, asleep on the cushion; and they woke Him and said to Him, 'Teacher, do You not care that we are perishing?' And He got up and rebuked the wind and said to the sea, 'Peace, be still.' And the wind died down, and it became perfectly calm." (Mark 4:37-39)*

In this passage, Jesus and His disciples were on a journey by boat when they unexpectedly encountered a storm at sea. This is no different than the storm of life that can suddenly impact us when we are on our way to a destination. We have a beautiful life planned out, and then boom! Adversity happens. This can come in the form of the loss of a job, a breakup with a lover, death, or any kind of loss or trauma. These all can be equated to the waves beating against the ship. Pay attention to what the great mastermind, the God consciousness, did. He didn't worry or panic. In fact, He was sleeping comfortably in the middle of the storm, just Him and His pillow. The wind was blowing, the boat was rocking, waves loudly beat against the ship, the boat was filling with water, the disciples were panicking, and yet, He was so deeply asleep with His pillow that He had to be awakened and asked if He even cared.

Notice what the great mastermind did next. He got up and rebuked the wind, the unseen. He didn't address the water that was filling the boat and beating it up but the cause of the raging sea. He did not jump up, panicking and screaming, "What are we going to do now?! We're all going to die! God, why did you let this happen to me? Where are you?" Jesus was conscious of the power within Him and used it. The water (seen) was an effect of the wind (unseen). He got up and said, "Peace, be still," and there was a great calm.

When you are feeling like you are caught in the middle of a storm, know that all is well and say, "Peace, be still." You have to be consistent through the chaos. Stand on the truth. As discussed in the previous chapter, Jesus used the law of confession to change the circumstances, but He used it to attack the unseen. We have to do the same. Once we have trained ourselves to think correctly and have better thoughts, our words will possess the power to change our circumstances in an instant. We will then have the power to harness peace and calm through a storm, with no sleepless nights. If you suffer from insomnia or some form of sleeping disorder, then you need to learn how to calm your mind. Your condition is a result of overthinking, fear, and worry. What's happening on the outside (seen) is just a reflection of what's going on inside (unseen). Sound sleep is a result of peace. You are a child of God, and a child deserves sleep. It is promised to you.

"It is vain for you to rise up early, to retire late, to eat the bread of painful labors; for He gives to His beloved even in His sleep." (Ps. 127:2)

Don't be hard on yourself. It is quite possible that you have been thinking negatively for a very long time, so don't expect overnight results. It is going to take some work to reverse your beliefs and way of thinking. Let's visit the stick figure below to give you some basic understanding of how the mind works so you can change your belief system, which will then change your actions, results, and the outer world.

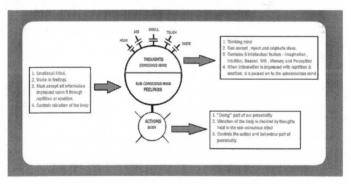

Diagram 2
http://bobproctorlessons.blogspot.com

You have a conscious and a subconscious mind. Your conscious mind is where an idea is built. It's what houses all of your natural senses—touch, smell, sight, hearing, and taste. It's what gives you the ability to accept or reject an idea. Your subconscious mind is home to your belief system. This is what controls your life. It doesn't have the ability to accept or reject ideas. It cannot take a joke. It accepts whatever is given or presented to it. This is why it can be programmed, and this is where your mental programming takes place. This programming often occurs at a young age. Most experts say the most critical periods of learning for a child occur between birth and seven years of age. Once you understand this, you can begin to raise your children totally different. You'll most likely become wary of exposing them to the music, TV shows, or adult talk they are currently exposed to. You may not think they are listening or have the ability to comprehend, but once you realize how the mind works, you will see this is far from the truth.

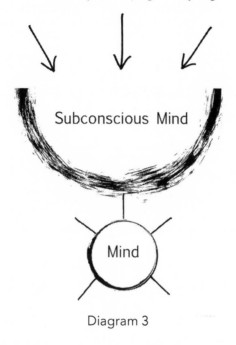

Conscious Mind is not developed..
The mind is open; accepting of everything.

Subconscious Mind

Mind

Diagram 3

A child's subconscious mind is totally open. In the diagram, we have removed the top half (the conscious) because it represents their mind being totally open, they do not have the mental capacity to accept or reject an idea; they don't know right from wrong. For instance, you can take a baby from America and put it in a household in China, and that baby will grow up speaking Chinese without any knowledge of the English language—and vice versa. You quite literally become a product of your environment. This is also why it is easier for a baby to learn multiple languages as opposed to a thirty-year-old adult. Children have no objections to what is being given to them. Adults, on the other hand, are filled with doubts, worries, and beliefs that don't even belong to them, as well as the programming from their childhood environment and their DNA. You are literally running around with other people's ideas in your head, which is why you have to be conscious of what is being offered to you. This is why you must renew your mind.

When ideas, whether your own or others', go into your conscious mind over and over again, they become planted in your subconscious mind. Those ideas, once planted, have the power to control your behavior. This is why repetition is a major key in learning something new. Contrary to popular belief, you don't learn by hearing or seeing something once. Think back to when you learned math or the alphabet. You practiced over and over again until it was programmed into your mind. Now, you can probably say the alphabet backwards if you had to. Your mind will start to believe whatever is repeatedly presented to it.

Do you remember when you first started driving? You most likely sat up straight with both hands on the wheel, paying attention to all the signs. You were probably conscious of every little thing around you. Now, you have been driving for awhile, perhaps daily. At this point, you do it without consciously thinking; you probably have your seat leaned back while you drive with one hand, and you may text at the same time or drive with your knees while you eat (none of which I condone). You are now driving from your subconscious. You can drive without thinking. I have actually fallen asleep while driving before, and I know for a fact only the power within kept me safe and between the lines. This is how it works with everything you do. Your subconscious controls your life. Once an idea is impressed through your conscious mind into the subconscious mind, it is expressed through the body.

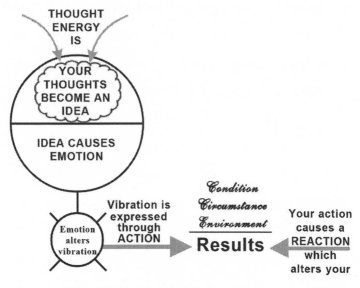

Diagram 4
https://www.proctorgallagherinstitute.com

The body is an instrument of the mind, so when negative thoughts and feelings take over, you feel worry, fear, and doubt. These thoughts are expressed through your body as anxiety, depression, or dis-ease because you think your needs won't be met. You have two brains: the thinking brain (conscious) and the emotional brain (subconscious), and the Centers for Disease Control (CDC) reported that 90% of disease is emotionally based.

"My people shall perish for lack of knowledge" (Hosea 4:6). This may sound harsh, but the polar opposite of knowledge is ignorance. Nine times out of ten, cases of anxiousness, depression, or misfortune are a product of ignorance. Saying that anxiety or disease comes from ignorance may offend some, but it will bless many more. If your world is turned upside down and you can't find anything positive in your outside world, you must understand how to build positivity from within. This is why affirmations and visualizations are so powerful. Through repetition, you can use these tools to impress positive ideas into your subconscious mind. Your thoughts and feelings become positive from knowing and internalizing that all things are provided and all is well. This belief comes from repeatedly studying, which brings knowledge and, eventually, understanding. "In all thy getting, get understanding" (Prov 4:7). Then faith can be manifested through the body as health, wealth, and well-being.

Ignorance	Knowledge
Worry/Doubt	Understanding
(think your needs won't get met)	(all things provided; gained through studying)
Fear	Faith
Anxiety	Well-being
Depression	Health/Wealth
(mental or physical) Dis-ease	At ease
Deceleration	Acceleration
Disintegration	Creation

Diagram 5

"Study to shew thyself approved unto God..." (2 Tim.2:15)

"A man's mind may be likened to a garden, which may be intelligently cultivated or allowed to run wild; but whether cultivated or neglected, it must, and will, bring forth. If no useful seeds are put into it, then an abundance of useless weed seeds will fall therein, and will continue to produce their kind."

—James Allen

You will be offered things, "useless weed seeds," as James Allen called it. It may sound crazy, but voices will speak to you. People try to act like hearing voices is just for the mentally insane, but the mind is constantly offered suggestions. Everything is after your mind, including phrases like "You're too young," "You're too old," "You're too dark," "You're too light," "You're not good enough," and so on. If you don't control what your mind hears, someone else will, and in a sense, they will control you.

> *"I can't stop birds from flying over my head, but I can stop them from building a nest."*
>
> *—Kenneth Hagin*
> *(referring to thoughts)*

If you are going to be a master, you have to discipline your hearing and sight. I listen to positive audiobooks all day. I don't even mind sitting in traffic anymore because it's a time for me to learn, an opportunity to sit, listen, and train my mind. I wouldn't dare give the radio that opportunity. Positive audiobooks are also a good cure for road rage. They help you maintain your control and your power. You have to train yourself to still those voices. Who are you listening to? Be still, and know that I am God. Say, "Peace, be still." Say "I am…" followed by the positive version of whatever lie or piece of negativity is being offered to you. Don't waste anymore time listening to or watching bad news. Don't waste anymore time with doubts and worries. "Let us go up at once and possess the promise!" (Num. 13:30).

If you find doubt, fear, and negativity in your mind, go up at once and possess it. Stop the voices of doubt, fear, and negativity immediately! Conscious awareness gives you the ability to recognize these thoughts and determine whether they serve you or not. Once you become consciously aware, you'll know what's a lie and what shouldn't be allowed to take root in your mind's beautiful garden.

> *"…the seed is the word of God."*
> *(Luke 8:11)*

This is why you always want to speak and think positively and only envision the outcomes you desire. Always believe that something wonderful is happening. Remember, whatever is impressed has to be expressed. Impress goodness, love, health, joy, success, peace, and happiness into your mind. Whatever you recognize, you energize. Stop recognizing the bad and your failures because you are only giving them power and energy. Never joke about yourself or say things, like "I'm so forgetful," "I'm so dumb,""I'm poor," "I'm broke," "I'm getting old," "I am just dying to go," or reply with "Dead" during a text conversation. How many of these things do you say without even realizing it? The subconscious mind doesn't understand jokes, and it catches everything. It is a listener and a believer. It will believe and act in accordance with anything it repeatedly hears to try and manifest it, good or bad. These subtle things can keep you from your destiny or even delay it. This concept even applies to anti-aging efforts.

Youthfulness is a state of mind. Don't talk or think about yourself as an old, feeble being. Never agree with being old, weak, or decayed. I hear people all the time say they can't physically do something because they are getting old or they are over the age of thirty. I even hear people say their memory is not what it used to be. Believe it or not, these are all choices. With age, you are made to be faster, mentally sharper, and physically stronger. You only get old because that's what you say and think. "As a man thinketh in his heart, so is he." If you think you're going to get old at thirty, then take a good guess at what's going to happen at thirty right on cue, just as you expected. The universe will ensure what you say comes to pass by any means. The subconscious is listening and is a willing servant. There is a God in you who doesn't forget, who isn't weak, and who doesn't decline with age.

> *"Finally, brethren, whatever is true, whatever is honorable, whatever is right, whatever is pure, whatever is lovely, whatever is of good repute, if there is any excellence and if anything worthy of praise, dwell on these things." (Phil. 4:8)*

Peace, Joy, and Happiness

"The steadfast of mind You will keep in perfect peace, because he trusts in You." (Isa. 26:3)

"You will have as much joy and laughter in life as you have faith in God."
—Martin Luther

If you don't have perfect peace, it's because your mind isn't focused on good and you don't trust in good. What you focus on is the key to your peace and happiness. To overcome fear, anxiety, and depression, you must learn to trust in love, to keep your mind focused on love and creation. You have been given a choice—blessing or curse, life or death. The power is within you. To sit around and think and accept the same miserable thoughts that are offered to you over and over again is lazy. To imagine the worst possible outcome that hasn't happened is almost insanity, especially once you find out the choice is yours to think better thoughts. The choice is yours to make better use of your imagination. These choices help shape the outcome. The same energy it takes to imagine the worst-case scenario is the same energy you can use to imagine it happening just the way you desire. Isn't that much more enjoyable? Go to your happy place in your mind as a child would. Once you learn how to believe, speak, and think properly, you will have peace and joy everlasting.

We often put our happiness off on future events, saying things like,"I will finally be happy when I get a new car/new house/more money." You are actually saying to yourself and the universe that you are not currently happy because things aren't how you want them. Saying you don't have enough is going to attract more unhappiness and lack. One of the main reasons anyone wants better health or a better job, car, or house is because they think it will make them happier than they currently are. So the trick is to be grateful and happy first, then the things that make you happy will appear.

> *"For whoever has, to him more shall be given, and he will have an abundance; but whoever does not have, even what he has shall be taken away from him." (Matt.13:12)*

You have to be happy now for more to come to you. Remember, you can only attract what you are. This is basically the same principle as the Law of Attraction. Once you have it, more will be given. If you feel bad, sad, anxious, or depressed, then that's all you can attract. So if you want more happiness, peace, and joy, you have to learn how to be happy, peaceful, and joyous in the present moment. You may ask, *How is that possible when I am feeling bad?* Speak! Call those things that are not as if they are.

The universe will set itself into motion to do all it can to make sure your word does not return void. When you are weak, say, "I am strong." Constantly affirm to yourself that you are strong. "I am peace;" "I am happy;" "I am healthy;" "I am wealthy." If you have a dog and it isn't where you want it to be, what do you do? You don't sit there, get frustrated, and complain that the dog isn't there. You call it until it comes. If the dog is already there, you are going to look pretty ridiculous calling for it to come. The same thing applies here: Call for your blessings until they come! Every morning, before you get out of bed, confess,"The joy of the Lord is my strength." What you do immediately after you wake up sets the tone for your day. Stop reaching for your phone as soon as you get up; there is no peace there.

> *"Seek ye first, the kingdom of God and His righteousness and all these things shall be added unto you."*
> *(Matt. 6:33)*

Instead, quiet your mind through prayer and meditation and give thanks for health, peace, joy, love, happiness, success, and prosperity. Affirm and visualize everything good you desire. Let go of worry and fear because no mind can create when it is divided against itself. Worry and fear also weaken the immune system. To be happy and joyous is good for your health.

In essence, joy and happiness are two separate things. Joy is the fruit of the spirit, which means if you have the spirit of God within you, joy is within you at all times. It is much more deeply rooted and stable than happiness. As you know, happiness can come and go, depending on the circumstances. This is why you never want to let anyone or anything steal your joy. Joy can literally strengthen you.

> *"...for the joy of the Lord is your strength." (Neh. 8:10)*

Renowned neurosurgeon Dr. Avery Jackson often conducts laughing classes for cancer patients. It has been proven in recent research that, with laughter and exercise, the body can repair itself. Dr. Jackson said, "God built in mechanisms to heal our imperfect, earthly bodies. Laughter is one of them." No matter what we are going through, we can make a conscious decision to laugh daily. Sometimes we have to stir up the joy that is down in our heart. It has been proven that the body doesn't know the difference between a genuine belly laugh and a fake laugh. You can literally trick yourself into being happy by stirring up that joy.

You can laugh, even when you don't feel like it. Start with just saying, "Ha, ha, ha," and as you keep doing it, watch your spirits lift and feel yourself break into "real" laughter. Have you ever noticed how contagious laughter is? Have you ever started laughing just because someone else was? They may not have even started speaking, but you are both laughing, having a good time, and you don't know why. The spirit of joy spreads very quickly. This is why the Good Book instructs you to count on joy when trouble comes.

Well, what is there to be joyous about when my world is crumbling around me? Research has found that laughter can improve your health and prevent disease by increasing blood flow, lowering blood pressure, releasing muscle tension, increasing feel-good hormones (dopamine and endorphins), decreasing stress hormones, boosting the immune system, burning calories, and giving an overall sense of well-being. "A joyful heart is good medicine, but a broken spirit dries up the bones" (Prov. 17:22). Joy is good for your health.

> "Therefore you will joyously draw water from the springs of salvation." (Isa. 12:3)

> "This is the day that the Lord has made. Let us rejoice and be glad in it." (Ps. 118:24)

Being happy is a sign of fulfillment. Sadness is a sign of lack. Over and over, you are given the benefits of joy, but you must put in the effort to maintain and protect what already belongs to you. Learn how to be disciplined enough to speak right, think right, and laugh, no matter how things look or feel. Now that you know the truth, you can be free, full of peace, love, joy, and happiness.

> "May you always remember to enjoy the road, especially when it's a hard one."
> —Kobe Bryant

Faith/Belief

"It shall be done to you according to your faith." (Matt. 9:29)

"Whether you think you can or you think you can't, you're right."
—Henry Ford

Now that you know who you are, have a visual of the mind, and can think and speak positively, you must learn about faith and belief. Knowing who you are helps you strengthen your faith.

"There is no fear in love; but perfect love casts out fear, because fear

involves punishment, and the one who fears is not perfected in love." (1 John 4:18)

We have already established that our true nature is love. God is love, and God is within us. We are made in His image of love. Fear and love cannot exist in the same space. As we saw in Diagram 5, fear and faith are polar opposites. Generally speaking, doubt and worry are the causes of fear. And anxiety, depression, and dis-ease are all manifestations of that fear just as well-being, peace, and joy are manifestations of faith, and are results of positive thinking, belief, and love. A lack of knowledge and fear is what makes the mind or body sick. Faith has the ability to make the body well and keep it well. When you study, you gain knowledge, and with knowledge comes understanding. Once you understand, faith comes, and once you have faith, you can overcome the world's challenges, including anxiety, depression, and sickness.

You may ask, *OK, what do I need to have faith in?* The answer is simple: Have faith in God, in love, and in the idea that He will never leave or forsake you. Have faith that He wouldn't mismanage your life. Would you want your child sick or depressed? No? Well, neither does the Heavenly Father. But the choice has been given to you. "… This day, choose who you will serve …" (Josh. 24:15). Part of your divinity is your power of choice—blessing or curse, life or death. Choose to walk with love. Choose to think with love. Choose life and blessings.

> "…I have set before you life and death, the blessing and the curse. So choose life in order that you may live, you and your descendants." (Deut. 30:19)

Have faith in good. Focus on good and focus on love. God is good, so to be good, you have to walk with God. No matter how your situation may look, always believe something wonderful is going to happen. I understand that may seem challenging or even impossible, depending on what phase of growth you are in right now.

> "….All things are possible to him who believes." (Mark 9:23)

How can you believe and have faith? Well, the first thing you want to do is pay attention to how you are feeling. Your feelings are an indication of what you have been thinking. What have you been paying attention to? Faith comes from hearing. What do you listen to on a regular basis? Do you allow your mind to wander? What kind of conversations do you entertain? Do you scroll through social media all day? If you are suffering from anxiety, depression, or any other ailment, you have to diligently tend to your mind's garden. Those are just external symptoms letting you know that you need to fix something on the inside. You need to change your belief system or way of thinking. Get all of the weeds out, all of the negative thoughts that don't align with love or your purpose, and began to think with intention. Only deposit thoughts of health, peace, joy, success, faith, and love into your mind. This sowing and reaping is a universal law; you get back what you put in.

Now that you know better, it is time to do better. Now the real fun can begin. Become consciously aware of your thoughts in every moment; think intentionally. I've heard it said many times that fear is inevitable; you just have to manage it or fight through it, but that is far from the truth. Fear has torment. There is no way a good father would want to torment his children. This is why He tells us, "Cast all your anxiety on Him because He cares for you" (1 Peter 5:7). Love doesn't want you anxious, depressed, or fearful. He would rather carry those burdens than His child. Perfect love casts out fear. You don't have to live with fear. You just have to be trained to think positively so you can control how you feel.

Do you think a window washer, a member of a bomb squad, or a firefighter wake up every day in fear of their job? Absolutely not! They have put their trust in something greater than what they are facing. The repetition of drills and training have altered their belief system. They have been given the knowledge or understanding to overcome the dangers of their job in the same way I have given you some fundamentals of overcoming your challenges. You can't believe beyond what you know, so studying is important. If you are stuck in a situation or a feeling, it's because you don't know how to get out of it. Learn how to rise above. Over and over, we are instructed to not be afraid. Fear not!

> *"He will not fear evil tidings; his heart is steadfast, trusting in the LORD."*
> *(Ps. 112:7)*

What you believe or have faith in controls your life. The subconscious mind is where your beliefs are stored. This is why we must monitor what ideas and images are being impressed to us because, with the power of repetition, your belief can be shaped or changed. The Bible tells us over and over again, "As a man thinks, so is he." Whatever you constantly think about, you become and attract. Do you have more faith in what you see or more faith in your promises?

> *"For God has not given us a spirit of timidity, but of power and love and discipline." (2 Tim. 1:7)*

The Best Ride Home Ever

It was the end of November, and the time had come to visit my family in Chicago for Thanksgiving. I was living in California at the time, and my presence was pretty much demanded at family gatherings, so I was always expected to fly in for all of the holidays and events. "If Courtney doesn't show up, then something has to be wrong." Not only that, but this time, a special family member was coming to town whom I hadn't seen in awhile, so I definitely had to be there. I wouldn't dare miss seeing them if I had the opportunity to; there was no excuse. Not to mention, being alone in my apartment during the holidays while everyone else was fellowshipping and feasting was the last thing I wanted. The only issue was I was in between work assignments, and I really didn't have the extra money to travel at the time. Ticket prices were unusually high, and it seemed as if someone from back home was calling daily to see what day I was arriving. As a result of my prior inner knowledge and faith training, even against all odds, I didn't panic because I quickly recognized the play.

Star football player Tom Brady once said, "I have the answers to the test now. You can't surprise me on defense; I've seen it all. I've processed 261 games; I've played them all. It's an incredibly hard sport, but because the processes are right and in place, for anyone with experience in their job, it's not as hard as it used to be. There was a time when quarterbacking was really hard for me because you didn't know what to do. Now, I really know what to do; I don't want to stop now. This is when it's really enjoyable to go out."

Like Brady, I knew the time had come for me to test my faith and knowledge. I had no money to travel over 2,000 miles away from home, and my phone was constantly ringing as the clock counted down to Thanksgiving. I realized there was no way a God of love would want me to miss that time with my family; He would want me to be reunited with them instead of being alone for the holidays. I believed it. As the week of Thanksgiving approached, I completely locked in. I stayed calm, monitored my thoughts, feelings, and emotions, and only envisioned and spoke the way I wanted the story to end.

That Tuesday, I specifically remember sitting on my front porch and getting calls from my mom and other family members asking if I was coming. Without knowing how I was going to get there and with only forty-eight hours left until the big day, I felt it in my spirit to confidently say, "Yes!" The questions kept coming: "What time do you want us to pick you up from the airport?" Talk about pressure, right? I never let it get to me, though. I had already cast my care, and I had left it in loving hands. Some may look at it as lying to my mom. "Don't you have to tell it like it is?" Well, if you tell it like it is, that's how it will remain. Faith calls things that are not as if they are.

Later that night, I received a call from a close friend who also lived in California. He told me he was leaving the next day to go to Chicago for the holidays. He informed me that he was riding with his business partner, who had a pair of toddlers his grandparents hadn't seen before. His grandparents happened to be in Chicago; it wasn't his hometown, but that was where he would be spending the holidays. My friend informed me that they were taking a private jet, and it would only be him, his business partner, and the two kids on the flight. The jet was a twelve seater, so there was plenty of room for me. My friend still needed to ask if it was OK that I tagged along, considering his business partner was very particular about who was around his children—understandable.

Nonetheless, he offered to see if I wanted to hitch a ride with them. Imagine that: hitchhiking a ride in a private jet across the country. I remained calm and focused as I waited for the verdict from the man. As an act of faith, I even packed my bags as if the trip was already confirmed. I didn't get a call back until the next day, with under an hour left before they were scheduled to leave. I was confirmed! I called my family and said I was on the way. I had to stunt a little and tell them, "You can pick me up from the private terminal at Midway." Not only did my faith provide me a ride home, but it did so in the most luxurious way possible—one round-trip flight from L.A. to Chicago on a private jet! Just for context, I would estimate that flight to be around sixty thousand dollars.

You have to exercise your faith, just like any physical muscle. If you don't use it, you'll lose it. When there is adversity or an obstacle, you should be happy and start rejoicing because you now have the opportunity to exercise, to get stronger and wiser. When you are expecting goodness, your faith cannot waver. Notice in my story, I didn't let my circumstances move me from what I believed. I kept everything in line with good. When those voices come asking, "What are you gonna do now? How is this going to happen?" you have to learn how to replace doubts and limiting beliefs with the truth. Learn how to deny the senses and refuse to quit. Stand on the truth. But to stand on the truth, you have to know the truth. That is the secret to faith. I will admit, that came with years of experience and training, but with coaching and practice, you can experience freedom and life more abundantly through a life of faith and love.

> *"Great faith comes out of great trials and tests. You will never have great faith without trials and tests."*
> —*Smith Wigglesworth*

"Say to those with an anxious heart, 'Take courage, fear not...'" (Isa. 35:4)

"Do not let your heart be troubled; believe in God..." (John 14:1)

"...Blessed are they who did not see, and yet believed." (John 20:29)

"...Do not be afraid any longer, only believe." (Mark 5:36)

"But when Jesus heard this, He answered him, 'Do not be afraid any longer; only believe, and she will be made well.'" (Luke 8:50)

"Do not fear, for I am with you; do not anxiously look about you, for I am your God; I will strengthen you, surely I will help you, surely I will uphold you with My righteous right hand." (Isa. 41:10)

Boot Camp According to Your Faith

In January 1998, I was in U.S. naval boot camp at the Great Lakes Naval Base, about an hour north of Chicago. If you know anything about January in Chicago, you know that zero degrees is a pretty normal temperature. On top of that, there is a windchill factor, which could make it feel like forty below zero. Nevertheless, in January, you can guarantee it will be cold.

One night, as we were getting ready to get into our bunks, the drill sergeant instructed us to open every other window in the building. We reluctantly did what we were told. It was either that or pay the price with some push-ups. It was freezing outside, and they wanted us to open every other window? I thought to myself, *This is beyond some boot camp punishment; this has to be inhumane. It's going to be freezing in here all night. We will never get any sleep.* Either the drill sergeant heard the murmurs around the room or he knew what we were thinking because he yelled out, "Quit your whining and go to sleep. I am doing you idiots a favor. There's fifty bodies sleeping in one area; I'm sure someone will be coughing all night. If we don't let air circulate, there is a great chance that one will get everyone sick. The windows are open to let the germs out. Besides, cold air doesn't make you sick, you idiots. Bundle up and go to sleep."

I had what they call an "ah-ha" moment or an epiphany. He uprooted my entire previous belief system. I thought for sure all that cold air blowing around would give me a cold and make me sick. It wasn't the cold air that would've made me sick but the *belief* that it would, just like how some believe traveling on airplanes or going outside with your hair wet will make you sick. These are all someone else's beliefs. They are far from the truth. The truth is none of those things have dominion over our perfect spirit. It's all according to your faith. If you believe traveling gets you sick, so be it. If you believe wet hair and cold air gets you sick, then it is so. Now that I believe none of these things affect my health, I am not subject to it, meaning I don't get sick—ever, not even a common cold! I know the power inside of me is far greater than any virus or ailment. You, too, can achieve this level of divine health.

Victory (All Is Well)

Know that all is well. God is with you. He will never leave you or forsake you. You may ask, "How can you be sure? If so, I wouldn't be in my condition." God never changes. It is you that got off of the path of love and illumination and wandered into the wilderness of fear, doubt, and unbelief. If God were to wander off into the wilderness with you, you wouldn't know what alignment is. You wouldn't appreciate the light, true love, and goodness as much. Most importantly, don't beat yourself up for wandering off the path; it's part of your journey. Sometimes the experience and journey is all you really wanted, anyway. Be kind to yourself because if you didn't know what it felt like to be out of alignment, you wouldn't know how good clarity feels. Simply put, if you didn't have cold, rainy days, you wouldn't appreciate the sunny beach days.

When you know who you are, the challenges of life cannot touch you. Knowing who you are puts you in harmony with victory and well-being. Knowing gives you the faith, patience, and understanding to endure until the victory. Anything you need in this world is already here and provided for you—health, peace, joy, love, success, and prosperity. Whether or not you see it in your life is up to you.

What loving parent wouldn't have things prepared for their child? When a woman becomes pregnant, preparations are made long before the child's arrival. The woman's body produces more nutrients for the baby, and her breasts even fill up with milk so the baby has food available upon entry into this world. The home is prepared with clothes, toys, a crib, or anything else she thinks the baby may need. Your Heavenly Father has prepared the earth for you in the same way. Just as that child has to learn how to crawl, walk, and speak, you, too, have to be born again and learn the right way to walk and talk in love. You have to learn how to see yourself how God sees you. He sees His child being faithful, believing, joyous, victorious, successful, healthy, wealthy, and free.

You are made in God's image.
You are made in Love's image.
You are made in the Creator's image.
You are made in a wonderful image.
You are made in the image of peace.
You are made in the image of grace.

I could go on forever, but that's what you should see. That's how you should act, think, and feel. You are made in His image, so you should look, act, speak, and stand just like your Father. There is no such thing as an incurable disease with God, the Good, the Creator. "Is anything too hard for God?" (Gen. 18:14).

Master the fundamentals, and master executing them. When you see a champion in sports, what you are seeing is someone or a team that has mastered the fundamentals. The fundamentals of being victorious in life involve positive thinking, speaking, hearing, seeing, believing, faith, and love. Once you master those, you will surely walk in victory, no matter the situation. One thing about being victorious or overcoming is you have to engage in some type of battle, game, or competition. This means there will be adversity and challenges, but the secret is when there is a problem, we have the advantage. I like to call it practice; it gives me the opportunity to work on what I have learned.

From my experience, the moment you think you have learned something, life will test you on it. When this happens to me, I always see it as a chance to see what I'm really made of. Great victories come from great battles. No fighter ever became a champion without great battles. In the military, you climb up the ranking and chain of command faster when you go to battle. This may be part of the reason why we are called to count on joy when the pressures of life arise. This is why we are supposed to always be in good cheer because we are overcomers and more than conquerors. We have to be aware that we always win in the end, no matter what. If you haven't seen the victory yet, then you're not at the end.

One last thing: None of this works if you have unforgiveness in your heart; your prayers will fall on deaf ears.

> *"Whenever you stand praying, forgive, if you have anything against anyone, so that your Father who is in heaven will also forgive you your transgressions." (Mark 11:25)*

You need to forgive anyone who may have done you wrong. To overcome any ailments, fear, anxiety, or depression, you have to let go of any resentment toward anyone or anything, including yourself. It's not for them but for you and your well-being. Remember, perfect love casts out fear. To walk with love, you must forgive.

Thank you for reading
Know Who You Are:
A Spiritual Guide to Eraticating,
Anxiety, Depression, and Dis-ease
If you enjoyed this book, please
leave an online review.

**KEEP IN TOUCH WITH
COURTNEY MARTIN**

Website: www.mycourtvision.com
Instagram: @KingCourt
Facebook: Courtney Martin
Twitter: KingCourt3

Made in the USA
Middletown, DE
21 September 2020